Praise for
Love Me In: A Sacred Pregnancy Journal

Simple tools like this pregnancy journal by Donna Seegers Abler are needed for these overwhelming times to support parents to have the best possible start when beginning or expanding a family.

—Kate White, MA, BCBMT, RCST®, CEIM, SEP, PPNE

"Love Me In: A Sacred Pregnancy Journal" is inspired! It provides an opportunity for prospective and expecting parents to go deeply within their hearts and minds as they bring new life into the world. From moments prior to conception to those precious few moments of holding their baby in their arms, parents are encouraged to consciously reflect and to share their own insights, wisdom, and love.

—Susan Highsmith, PhD, PPNE, author of *Renaissance of Love*

Donna taps into the mystery of our body, heart, and spirit to connect expecting parents to the depth of what takes place during conception, pregnancy, and birth. This wisdom gained will create empowerment and deep bonding with yourself and your babe. Donna helps you create this relationship that will be everlasting.

—Dr. Peg Bledsoe, OTD, OTR/L, FOATA, BPC

Love Me In

A Sacred Pregnancy Journal

Written by Donna Seegers Abler, OTR/L, PPNE

Illustrations by Marguerite Herbst

Copyright © 2021 by Donna Seegers Abler
All rights reserved.

No part of this book may be reproduced or used in any manner without written permission from the author.

Works by other authors used with permission.

Published by
HenschelHAUS Publishing, Inc.
www.henschelHAUSbooks.com
ISBN: 978159598-790-7
LCCN: 2020948200

Artwork by Sadie Rose Abler
Illustrations by Marguerite Herbst
Cover and title page design by Michelle Lawrence
Cover photo: Studio 29 Photography

This journal is dedicated to my amazing daughters,
Jenni, Sadie, Tess, Brigid, and Grace,
whom I have carried, birthed, or guided.

You have taught me much, helped me expand exponentially,
and reconnected me to my sentient, Spiritual Self.

With gratitude to all the babies from the Earth plane
and from the Spirit plane, especially Baby Anders,
who have guided and inspired this journal.

Foreword

Love Me In, an inspired title, is a gift for any woman thinking about pregnancy. She may be contemplating getting pregnant or she may be pregnant already. This journal gives her the opportunity to share her love with the essence of her Little One in a way that has not been encouraged before. The journal itself is an expression of the new paradigm in childbirth — it focuses on the voice of the child who is saying "Love me in!"

Here, expecting parents can have a conversation with their unborn child. They can feel the sacred spirituality inherent in being pregnant and connect with their inner knowing. Ancient traditions and modern science have been reminding us of what a mother knows in her heart: the child growing in her womb is a conscious being receiving her thoughts, her feelings, her love. Sharing her words on the pages of this journal builds bonds, supports development, and enhances the life of the precious soul she is welcoming in. Empowered by simple yet elegant practices suggested by the author, each mother will discover that she and her baby are sharing a journey that enriches them both.

—Susan Highsmith, PhD

Dear Amazing Beings!

I am passionate about empowering expecting parents to consciously guide and ease their babies into life. Our babies need us more than ever to be present and connected to our body and Divine self as they incarnate in our wombs and transition to Earth. I have worked with many newborns and children in my professional work whose transition was arduous and traumatic. And, I have dedicated extensive work understanding and healing my own deep emotional wounds and mindsets imprinted through my birth story.

I can't help but wonder what imprints are cast for babies who are welcomed in on a multi-dimensional structure with conscious honor, respect and unconditional love.

I envision an exciting new paradigm; a paradigm that is shifting to a greater interconnected, conscious world; a world that has as its core beliefs deep spiritual connection, unity, and the frequency of Heart-based Love.

What would happen in our world if every baby is wanted, freely chosen, nurtured, and loved into being, welcomed to Mother Earth unconditionally and intentionally?

Imagine yourself being on a sacred journey to guide and welcome in a beautiful sentient being who is conscious and aware prior to conception.

I invite you into your magnificent journey ahead to birth not just your physical baby, but to deeply bond with and birth your baby's essence with thoughtful, guided awareness; to birth a Spiritual being that vibrates with the Highest of Love, Joy and Happiness to support an awake, thriving and united Humanity.

Create time to use this journal as a guide to nurture and nourish yourself through your pregnancy. You deserve to be supported. Mamas, invite your partner or coach into this journey with you. This may be your husband, wife, soul sister, family member, doula, or pregnancy coach.

There are beautiful guided practices throughout the journal to create sacred space, develop ritual, reflect, connect with your inner self, embrace self-care, meditate and journal to enrich both you and your baby.

Allow yourself to receive Divine Love and guidance as you love yourself into parenthood and love your baby into being.

Blessings on your sacred journey!

Donna

First of three paintings in the "Head, Heart, Hands" series by Sadie Rose Abler

Contents

Sacred Ritual 3

Honoring the Female Body 11

Conscious Conception 25

Harmonizing Hearts 37

Water Your Womb 49

Prenatal Bonding 63

Calling in a Name 77

Mothering the Mother 81

References and Resources 103

About the Author 105

*No matter where you are in your pregnancy journey,
I encourage you to start at the beginning of this journal
and allow yourself to immerse into the sacredness of each step
along the way, being present with each phase and transition.*

*Your body can energetically process each section
regardless of how far you are in your pregnancy.*

Ritual is an action done with intention, presence and purpose to seek guidance, insight, transformation, or healing.

Sacred Ritual

Empowering Self and Connecting to
Your Innate Knowing

Sacred Space

I think of sacred space as a retreat place for stillness and seclusion from the noise of the external world. Many of us have become accustomed to the business and fast pace of everyday life, juggling the many needs of those around us, often putting our own needs last.

Sacred spaces can invoke beauty, peace, joy, reverence, and love through our senses and emotions. They can be external places, such as a place of worship, a beautiful landscape, a sparkling brook, a magnificent sunset, or an inspiring piece of music.

We also have the ability to create sacred space within ourselves. This requires a commitment of allowing time for ourselves to connect inward and become attentive and still to our own innate voice of our heart, sometimes called our inner wisdom.

Create your sacred space to return to throughout your pregnancy journey

- ♥ Sacred space can be very simple. The sacred space or altar acts as a container to help hold together the energy intention of a ritual.
- ♥ Consider a little desktop space or a specific sitting place in a room that gives you quiet, stillness, and peace to center within.
- ♥ A sacred space may contain items to represent beauty, peace, reverence, and love.
- ♥ You may feel called to a specific stone, picture, candle, or baby item that has meaning to you.

Steps of a Ritual

Personal ritual is a sequence of chosen practices or intentional habits to help draw us into our sacred space. Ritual can provide opportunity to gain clarity, meaning, and deeper purpose in life. It can restore harmony and balance. It can mark important events such as birthing a baby and transitioning to parenthood.

You will be invited to use ritual throughout your pregnancy to allow time for yourself, to connect with your inner heart knowing, to bond deeply with your baby and to gain confidence and trust in your pregnancy and birth.

Settle into your sacred space. Sit upright with your feet flat on the floor if your body allows. If not, find a position that supports your physical needs.

Pause, be still and breathe. Release the energy of the external world around you.

- ♥ Begin with an initial prayer or verse to speak aloud or in silence.
- ♥ Invite spirit guides and Divine presence into your space. This may be an angel, archangel, an ancestor, or your name for Divine One.
- ♥ Reflect and listen deeply to your inner heart's messages. Your heart may speak through visions, colors, symbols, sounds, sensations, stories, metaphors, or messages.
- ♥ Give thanks and gratitude for Divine guidance, insight, and renewal.
- ♥ Close your sacred space by blowing out a candle, ringing a chime, shaking a tiny baby rattle or singing a favorite lullaby.
- ♥ Use the journaling pages to record how ritual and guided practices shape your pregnancy and birth experience.

Journaling Reflections

Describe your sacred space and your initial experiences:

_____
_____
_____
_____
_____
_____
_____
_____
_____
_____
_____
_____
_____

Journaling Reflections

By exploring this place where the universal energy meets the female body, we come home to the mystery within us and engage with that mystery to give life to the body and body to the life.

—Tami Lynn Kent

Honoring Your Female Body

You are Blessed With an Amazing Female Body with a Womb Space to Create, Hold and Birth New Life

Feminine Body Blessing

We are amazing spiritual beings who chose to embody in physical from in our mother's womb. It's a wondrous mystery to incarnate into physical form.

The journey to earth and on earth can be difficult and stressful for many. Life can become so overpowering that we lose connection to ourselves and our wholeness. Perhaps we suffered trauma or life wounds that created a disconnect from our emotional, physical, or energetic bodies. Perhaps we were taught to not appreciate and love our bodies or acknowledge our own needs. Some may feel abandoned, unloved or unwanted, leaving a sense of deep betrayal.

I have experienced this struggle in my own birth story, as well as in my professional work with clients.

We know babies are sentient beings with awareness from preconception. The voices of incoming babies are asking their parents to be consciously present and connected during conception, pregnancy, and birth. They are asking to be loved, seen, heard, and welcomed unconditionally.

This **Female Body Blessing** is a beautiful ceremony inviting you, Mama, with the help of your partner or coach, to connect fully with your female body. The more present you are in your body, the more present you are for your growing baby.

Presence in your body can be difficult or feel unsafe, especially if you suffered trauma. Please consult a professional if you need further support.

Find some uninterrupted time for yourself and your partner or coach.

Settle into your sacred space and allow yourself to enjoy this beautiful feminine body blessing.

- ♥ Sit upright in a comfortable, supportive chair with your feet rooted on earth or find an alternate position for your physical body needs.
- ♥ Roll your shoulders back and open your chest.
- ♥ Put your hands on your womb space.
- ♥ Breathe deeply into your heart and belly.
- ♥ Allow your partner or support person to read aloud the **Wild and Feminine Body Blessing** on the next page.
- ♥ Go slowly. Pause after each phrase to honor the words.
- ♥ Send love to and bless each part of your beautiful sacred body.
- ♥ Give gratitude for your amazing body that can create, hold, and birth new life.

Wild and Feminine Body Blessing

Bless your feet and legs; let them walk with the grounding
energy of the earth.
Bless your pelvis, that you may hold your values as a woman,
make space for creation and release what no longer belongs with you.
Bless your vagina, may you be clear about what you bring into
or release from your body or life.
Bless your feminine organs, that you use your creative potential
in ways that are beneficial and sustainable for your spirit.
Bless your belly; may you be in your place of feminine power.
Bless your hands and arms; may they cultivate
and receive a joyful bounty.
Bless your heart and chest; that you receive
and give fully the love you share with others.
Bless your breasts; that you nourish yourself
as lovingly as you nourish your creations.
Bless your throat and head; may you speak your truth
and clarify your visions.
Bless the paths behind and ahead of you,
that they may transform what you carry into the future.
Bless the place you now stand as a woman;
may you be fully present in your body and life and
celebrate the blessings of this moment.
May you always remember your sacred bodies.

—Tami Lynn Kent

Journaling Reflections

How did it feel to honor your body in this blessing?

_____
_____
_____
_____

What emotions came up for you?

_____
_____
_____
_____

Are there any areas of yourself you'd like to give more attention to?

_____
_____
_____
_____
_____
_____

The Importance of Self-Care and Inner Connection

Pregnancy is an exciting time for expecting parents! It is a time of anticipation to meet your new little one. It is a time of creating dreams and hopes for the life you are creating. And, pregnancy can also bring overwhelm and stress with the demands of your continuously changing physical body, emotions, hormones, relationship and family needs, and pregnancy and birth plans.

Avoiding stress is a tremendous challenge in a non-stop, superwoman society. As mamas, we are often trained to take care of everyone else's needs around us before our own. Yet, to nurture a healthy pregnancy and prepare for motherhood, there is the need to create the groundwork to be connected to self.

In our Western world, expecting parents are trained to spend more focus on external physical ideas and intellectual concepts related to pregnancy. Less focus is given to mental, emotional and spiritual inner aspects of pregnancy.

Giving yourself permission for regular self-care practices is essential for a healthy pregnancy and infant bonding. Make time for yourself daily throughout your pregnancy even if it's just for a few minutes to breathe consciously and connect with your heart.

Healthy Self-Care Practices might include:

- ♥ Eating well
- ♥ Good sleep
- ♥ Physical movement
- ♥ Joyful play and laughter
- ♥ Renewal through nature, rest, music, art, etc.
- ♥ Practicing gratitude
- ♥ Conscious breathing
- ♥ Being mindful of your words and thoughts as they create energetic and neurochemical responses in your body
- ♥ Meditation to connect with your inner knowing from the guidance and wisdom of your heart

What would your body like today?

- ♥ Gentle yoga stretches
- ♥ A mindful walk
- ♥ Rejuvenating rest
- ♥ A hot, soaking bath
- ♥ Time in your sacred space
- ♥ A cup of tea

Settle into your sacred space.

- ♥ Allow yourself to be still and breathe into every inch of your body.
- ♥ Allow your breath to move in and out like a wave gently washing up to shore, gathering in the day's stresses and carrying them out into the great expanse of the ocean.
- ♥ Feel yourself become lighter with renewed strength.
- ♥ Feel love flowing into you and washing over every part of your being.
- ♥ Divine love accepts every part of you just as you are.
- ♥ Give gratitude for the amazing person you are!
- ♥ Give gratitude for the support of Divine Love.

Partner Support During Pregnancy

Relationship is a delicate dance between yourself and another. The dance involves many steps, such as connection, interaction, bonding, communication, commitment, safety, trust, giving, and receiving.

Our own patterns for relationship began in our in utero experience and continued to be shaped throughout our childhood. Families and society further influence our beliefs, experiences, and cultural ideas about relationship. Societal stereotypes continue to exist around male and female roles in relationship. Women often struggle with the role of caretaker, resulting in an imbalance of giving and receiving in relationship.

In pregnancy, your body is nurturing and creating new life in your womb. While it is a time of wonder and marvel, it can also be a time of uncertainty and unknown of many new experiences ahead.
Pregnancy and childbirth often bring up fears, anxiety, and concerns for the pregnant mama, such as "Will my baby be healthy?" and "Will I be strong enough for labor and delivery?"

It's important, mamas, to allow yourself to receive support during these big events in your life, whether or not you are in a partner relationship.

Reflection Exercise

Settle into your sacred space and spend time reflecting on your beliefs and experiences in relationship.

- ♥ If you are in partnership, discuss the journaling questions together.

- ♥ If you do not have a partner, communicate these ideas with your coach or support person.

Journaling Reflections

What were your early experiences with relationships?

_____
_____
_____
_____

How do you balance giving and receiving in relationships?

_____
_____
_____
_____

What do you see as your biggest needs for support during pregnancy and birth?

_____
_____
_____
_____
_____
_____

The Important Role of the Partner

♥ To become educated and understand the process of pregnancy and birth.

♥ To provide safety, support, and protection to the pregnant mama throughout pregnancy and birth.

♥ To explore the role of a doula or pregnancy coach.

Reflecting with Gratitude

Blessed is she who believes in herself.

Blessed is she who believes in her partner.

What are three things you love about yourself?

What are three things you love about your partner?

1. _____

2. _____

3. _____

1. _____

2. _____

3. _____

Embryologists have captured the moment of conception via florescent microscopy. They discovered that at the exact moment a sperm penetrates an egg, the egg releases billions of zinc atoms that emit light.

Sparks literally fly!

Conscious Conception

The Act of Creation When Egg and Sperm and Divine Energy Unite

The stars and the whole Universe collided to ignite your Divine Spark!

The Mystery of Conception

Science defines conception as the time when the sperm fertilizes the egg. But how is this fertilized egg imbued with spirit, our life force energy? And, what consciousness guides this incredible orchestration to form new life?

In the depths of meditation early one morning, I experienced my own conception and implantation. It was an incredible event that involved a consciousness beyond the physical world.

It appeared like this:

Flashes of magnificent light emerged from a distance. The light started as radiant white light pulsing with changing form and color. As the light got closer, brilliant hues of pinks and purples appeared. It was like a comet of energy coming in, imbued with life force and fluid swirls of cellular encoding. Closer and closer. More and more brilliant. There was an explosive flash! And then everything went dark and still and dense.

> *The 9 Months that Made You*
> is a remarkable PBS documentary showcasing breathtaking
> and exquisite imagery of the developing fetus
> from conception to birth. Take time to discover more about the
> mysteries of conception, pregnancy, and birth.

Journaling Reflections

Write the story of your baby's conception.

Dear Precious One,

Thank you for choosing to be conceived

and to add your Shining Light

into this World.

Settle into your sacred space and share these thoughts with your precious one:

- ♥ I/we are honored with whatever way you came into being, whether that was planned or unexpected, naturally conceived or medically assisted.
- ♥ I/we are honored you chose us as your parents.
- ♥ I/we are honored with all that you will teach us.
- ♥ I am honored to carry your essence within me.

Give honoring gratitude daily to your growing baby in your womb.

You are carrying a Being of Light
transforming into flesh.

Acknowledge and celebrate
the Divine Miracle you are carrying.
Honor the magnificent accomplishment of
conceiving, implanting, and cultivating your
beautiful baby within your temple.

Bless this new life with Divine Love
in every breath you take.
Love yourself.
Love your baby in.

> Embryological research indicates that as early as the 2-cell stage of development, the cellular receptors form a critical intrauterine growth hormone, IgF2. This hormone level can vary depending on the mother's emotional state.
>
> This variance imprints a differential message around growth potential in the first cell division.

Research on DNA cheek scrapings in vitro supports the same concept; a baby's cellular intelligence reads the environment and adapts to survive in that environment either by:

- ♥ growing to optimum potential, or
- ♥ protecting for safety.

Affirmations for Your Baby

Communicate with your baby to create an environment of love and safety. Speak reassuring messages to help your baby thrive.

Settle into your sacred space and spend time speaking these affirmations to your baby:

- ♥ You are loved and empowered to grow to optimal potential.
- ♥ The Universe orchestrates around you in a magnificent way for you to thrive.
- ♥ Your life purpose awaits your readiness to unfold.

Each life involves an essential errand;
not simply the task of survival, but a mission
imbedded in the soul from the beginning.

—Michael Meade

Dr. Masaru Emoto's research found that different kinds of thoughts influenced the molecular shape of water crystals.

Thoughts of truth, love, and gratitude produced organized, symmetrical, and beautiful growth patterns.

Did you know that a fertilized egg is 90% water?

Feed your fertilized egg with your positive thoughts of truth, love, and gratitude.

Loving Imprints

Settle into your sacred space for ritual. Reflect on the words and thoughts you want to imprint into your baby.

- ♥ Be still and breathe into the Divine Spark that has implanted in your womb. Surround it with Love and gratitude.
- ♥ Breathe into the idea that Sacred Knowledge and Divine Knowing are rooted in your baby's consciousness.
- ♥ Breathe into the idea that your baby's life purpose codes are tangibly available in his/her conscious mind to access after birth and throughout life on Earth.

Journaling Reflections

Your Heart contains your deepest treasures.

It carries your Love, Joy,
Courage, and Creativity.

It reveals your Soul's desire and purpose.

Connecting with your heart
opens every door
to your gifts.

The Beauty of the Heart

Many of us know the heart as the physical organ that circulates all the blood and oxygen in our bodies.

Our heart is also the center of our energetic self. The heart's energy field is about 60 times greater in amplitude than the electrical activity of the brain. It envelopes every cell and organ in the body. Our emotional state is encoded in the heart's magnetic field. The greater one develops their heart capacity, the greater one's qualities of beauty, gentleness, compassion, empathy and love.

And, our heart is the very core of who we are. It is the connection to our inner wisdom and infinite source. Our heart is the only organ that has a beat. We can learn to access our heart's deeper treasures by learning to bring awareness to our pulse and our heartbeat.

Listening to your heartbeat brings your mental focus to your inner voice.

Listening to Your Heartbeat

Settle into your sacred space.

- ♥ Pause and reflect on the magnificence of having two heartbeats (or more) in your body.
- ♥ Feel the power of multiple portals of Divine Love moving through you.
- ♥ Breathe and receive the Divine essence.
- ♥ Feel the Love.

Love is the very core of who you are.
Like your breath and your heartbeat,
Love is a constant that flows
through you.

Heartbeat Meditation

Your heartbeat and pulse attune your focus to your internal rhythm. They help to ground and anchor you in the present.

Settle into your sacred space.

- ♥ Get comfortable and sit upright in a supportive chair.
- ♥ Put your feet firmly on the ground with your pelvis tilted forward.
- ♥ Give your belly room to expand out.
- ♥ Sit with your back tall and your shoulders back.
- ♥ Gently breathe in and fill your belly with energized air.
- ♥ Breathe out and let your tummy fully sink in for a complete exhale.
- ♥ Breathe in for 4 counts.
- ♥ Breathe out for 6 counts.
- ♥ Listen for your heartbeat or feel for your pulse.
- ♥ Focus on stilling your mind and connecting your breath to your heartbeat.

Journaling Reflections

Reflect on the power of feeling your pulse and listening for your heartbeat.

_____
_____
_____
_____
_____
_____
_____
_____
_____
_____
_____
_____
_____
_____

Into my will, let there pour strength.
Into my feeling, let there shine light
that I may nurture this child
with enlightened purpose,
caring with heart's love
and bringing wisdom into all things.
—Rudolf Steiner

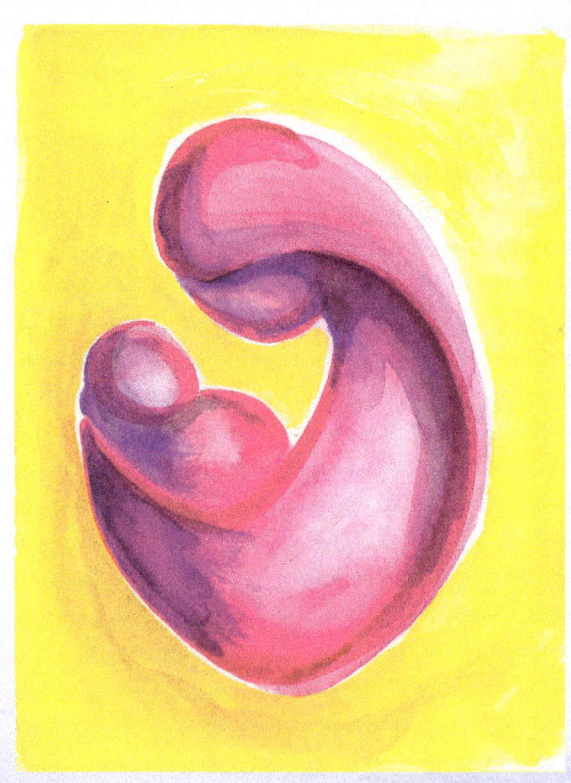

The fetal heart begins to beat at 18 to 22 days post-conception.

The tiny heart begins to pulse a rhythm that radiates Divine Love.

Harmonize Your Love Meditation

Settle into your sacred space.

- ♥ Sit up straight in a supportive chair.
- ♥ Bring your attention to allow your breath to flow in and out, washing over your body.
- ♥ Soothing. Calming. Quieting.
- ♥ Place one hand over your heart and feel for your heartbeat.
- ♥ Place another hand on your belly.
- ♥ Notice the sensations of your breath, your heartbeat, and your belly.
- ♥ Tune in to your baby.
- ♥ Sense your baby's heartbeat even if you don't feel or hear it.
- ♥ Listen deeply and breathe rhythmically.
- ♥ Breathe in and out in a figure-8 pattern, encircling your heartbeat with your baby's heartbeat.
- ♥ Let your heartbeats connect and synch together in love.

Journaling Reflections

What was your experience during this meditation?

Ultrasound Images
(Secure your images here)

Ultrasound Images
(Secure your images here)

As babies are growing in the womb,
their cells are aware of their environment
long before their brain develops.

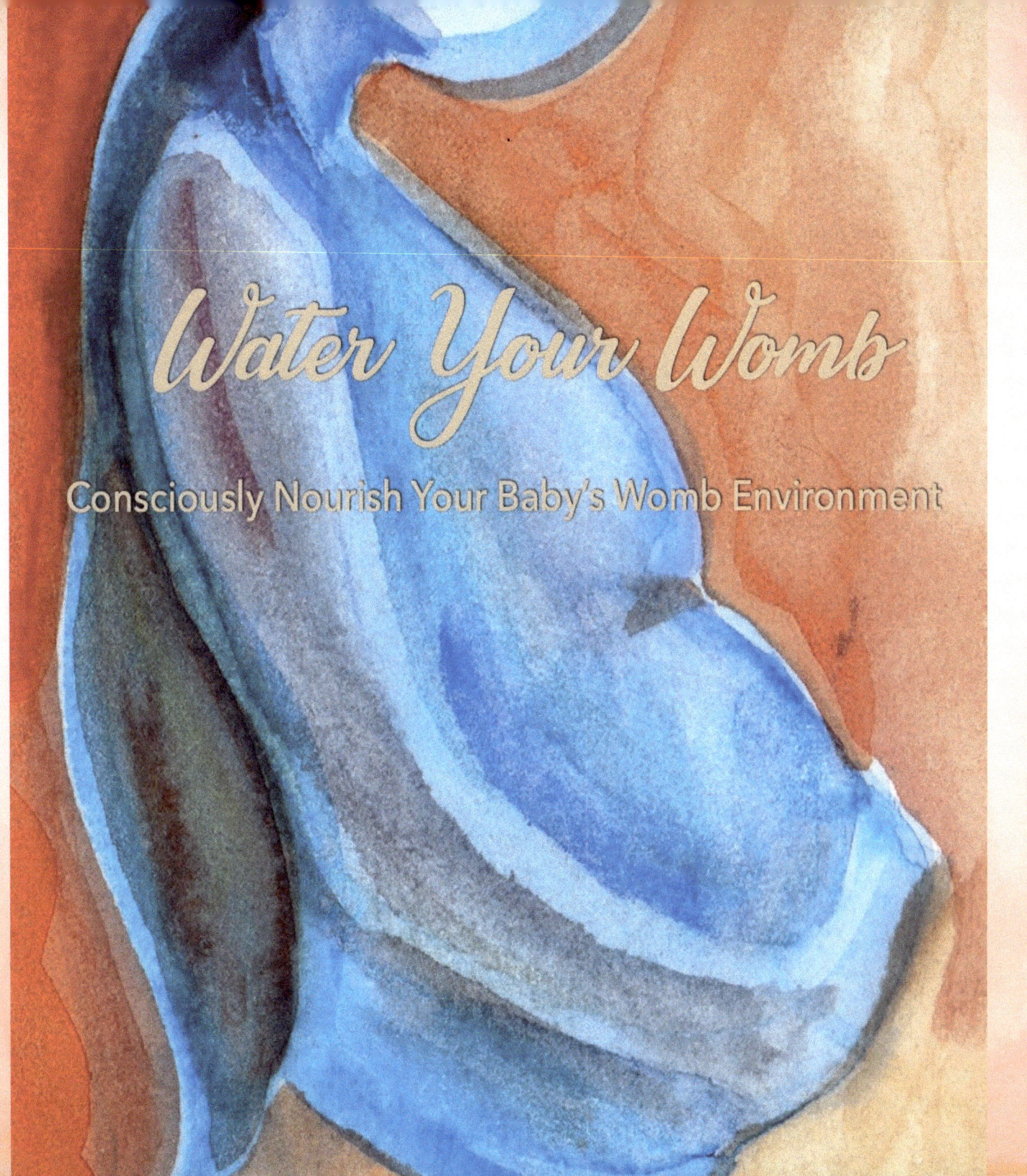

Nourishing Your Baby's Womb Environment

The more mindful you are about what you allow into your baby's environment, the healthier the outcome for your developing baby.

We now know that babies are an intricate part of their parents' emotional make-up, subconscious beliefs, and family lineage.

Theory and research from the past 20 years indicates that prenatal experiences in the womb can be remembered and have a life-long impact.

Spend time with your partner communicating and exploring how you were raised, your family beliefs, and your attitudes toward parenting and bringing a child into the world.

Some of these conversations may bring up uncomfortable feelings and childhood memories. Some may bring warm memories and gratitude for the caring and nurturing you received growing up.

Please seek additional counseling if significant challenges arise.

> "For healthy bonding and infant self-realization,
> the mother has to be in a healthy state of being
> as the baby resonates with and imprints its mother's state
> of being in utero."
>
> —Wendy Anne McCarty, 2009,
> *Welcoming Consciousness*

Settle into your sacred space.

- ♥ Reflect on mindsets that you and your partner carry about family, parenthood, and bringing a baby into this world.

Journaling Reflections

What beliefs and emotions sustain and nourish you and your baby?

_____
_____
_____
_____
_____
_____

What beliefs and emotions are limiting and need to be released?

_____
_____
_____
_____
_____
_____

Journaling Reflections

What parts of yourself were most accepted and nurtured growing up?

_____
_____
_____
_____
_____
_____
_____

What parts of yourself would you like to nurture and empower as you transition into parenthood?

_____
_____
_____
_____
_____
_____
_____

Water Your Womb with Practices to Support Your Baby

♥ Share with your baby what is happening in the environment around you. If a stressful event happens, let your baby know what is happening and reassure your little one that he/she is safe and is loved.

♥ Share loving messages every day with your baby. Pause for five minutes and connect deeply.

♥ Remember, your own self-care helps nourish your baby's environment. It is important to nurture your own body, heart, and soul every day.

Differentiation Exercise for Expecting Parents
—Kate White

We know stress impacts the developing baby in your belly. It is unrealistic to remove all stress from your life while you are pregnant. Differentiation as a simple tool helps relieve the stress that families feel and promotes connection with the developing baby.

Using this *Differentiation Exercise* can help your baby differentiate and know the stress is not about him/her.

Settle yourself as much as you can after a stressful event or day.

- ♥ Put your hands on your belly and say to your baby, either out loud or internally, "Wow, that was stressful."
- ♥ "That was not about you."
- ♥ Speak positive affirmations to your baby such as:
    - "I/We love you."
    - "I/We will keep you safe."
    - " I/We will protect you."

The Remembrance Process
Filling Up with Divine Love

The Remembrance Process was developed by Rita Kluny, founder of Healing Touch for Babies. It was created with the intention of helping parents remember their own inner source. This can support forming a life-long bond with their baby and preparing for Divine parenthood.

Settle into your sacred space.

- ♥ Sit comfortably in a supportive chair with your feet on the floor.
- ♥ Put your hand over your heart and focus your attention there.
- ♥ Set your intention to be held with Divine Love.
- ♥ Feel the rise and fall of your chest as you breathe. Notice any tension in your body.
- ♥ Allow yourself to relax.
- ♥ Begin to breathe directly from your heart forward right through your chest wall.
- ♥ Start repeating your name for Divine Presence or a word that makes you feel reverence, such as Divine, One Heart, or God.
- ♥ Slowly sense and receive the Presence.
- ♥ Continue to repeat the name or word to recognize the Love within you.

It is important to remember your own self-worth as you prepare to nurture this new being. Speak these words to yourself and your baby. Invite your partner to participate with you. Empower yourself.

Remember that you are worthy.

Remember that you are enough.

Remember that you are safe.

Remember that you are loved.

Remember that you ARE love.

Journaling Reflections

Journaling Reflections

I encourage you to take time and work deeply with the *Remembrance Exercise.*

Many people struggle internally with conflicts of being worthy, feeling like they are enough, that they matter and belong. These themes are deeply rooted in our society.

I experienced this in my own life journey and have treated these feelings in many clients throughout my career.

I particularly remember one little guy who transitioned to earth and was very disoriented after being separated from his mama. He was transferred to the neonatal intensive care unit after birth for breathing observation. Our Western medical model usually assesses breathing as a physical body medical concern.

The infant needed to be reminded that he belonged here and that he was safe and loved.

I wrote his story called *A Little Chat.*

A Little Chat

As I was making rounds early one morning in the neonatal intensive care unit, I followed a cry to the end of a row of three critical-care bed spaces.

The curtain was drawn for privacy and sensory protection. The lights were dimmed.

I approached the bed space just as the nurse tiptoed gingerly from behind the curtain. She looked relieved as I approached. She asked if I could do something to help console this baby.

I quietly stepped behind the curtain and listened deeply.

He was not from around here. This place was very foreign to him. I scooped him up with his permission. I acknowledged and reflected that he was from far, far away.

He quieted and stilled, blinking his wide, saucer eyes at me. His head was big and round and bald. I told him he was on Earth now. It was where he chose to come.

The infant listened and remembered and settled in.

The nurse peeked her head around the curtain, asking, "What did you do? That baby has not been quiet since he arrived."

I responded, "We just had a little chat."

—Donna Seegers Abler

The key to communicating
with the silent womb is
knowledge of what's going on there.
—Dr. David Chamberlain

Prenatal Bonding

Connecting With Your Baby's Developing Senses

Prenatal bonding and enrichment improves your baby's development and also begins the process of parent/child bonding.

> Research shows that babies who receive prenatal enrichment demonstrate superior fine and gross motor skills, earlier speech and language development, earlier smiling and greater contentment after birth, superior visual and auditory perception, and superior coordination and cognitive development.
>
> —Dr. David Chamberlain

Your baby is learning in your womb through its senses during your entire pregnancy. New studies indicate that babies form memories of their in utero learning.

I had a profound experience carrying my third child. While I was pregnant, I was consciously supporting my grandmother's crossing over to Spirit World.

I visited her often in the long-term rehabilitation center. We played cards, decorated her favorite sugar cookies, and had her hair done. Sometimes, I just sat quietly with her.

My daughter was born a couple of months after Grandma's passing. When my daughter started talking, she described clear and accurate images of being inside the rehab center visiting Grandma. One day, she asked me about my grandmother and called her by her first name, Cordula. The family never referred to Grandma by her first name.

"Cordula" means heart.

When we are connected by the Universal Heart, we sense into expanded consciousness.

—Donna Seegers Abler

The Sense of Touch

Touch is the first sensory system to develop in utero. The skin is our tactile organ. Fetuses experience touch in utero both from inside and outside the womb. Touch is the foundation of the sense of self. Respectful touch imprints the idea of, "I am a valuable person who has the right to be respected by others." It gives us a sense of a healthy boundary between ourselves and another.

Settle into your sacred space.

- ♥ Notice where your baby is positioned in your belly. Where do you feel your baby? Where is his/her head located? Where are the feet?

- ♥ What surfaces does he/she contact—your organs, ribs, pelvis, umbilical cord, placenta?

- ♥ Invite your baby to find a comfortable space inside your womb. Breathe into your womb spaces. Visualize gentle touch from within.

- ♥ Offer gentle touch massage to your belly to connect with your baby. Allow your partner to join you in belly massage to bond with your baby.

Journaling Reflections

How does your baby respond to touch input?

_____
_____
_____
_____
_____
_____
_____
_____
_____
_____
_____
_____
_____

The Sense of Smell

Between 6 and 8 weeks of pregnancy, neurons develop that help your baby's brain process odors. The two nasal cavities for the nose form.

> When that beautiful baby of yours is born, he or she will recognize you simply by your smell.

By 11 to 19 weeks of pregnancy, the scents a baby inhales can communicate with the brain.

By 4 to 5 months of pregnancy, your baby's little nose is ready to detect odors.

A number of studies also show that even the tiniest of newborn babies recognize their mothers by the smell of their skin and breast milk.

Journaling Reflections

The Sense of Movement & Balance

The vestibular sense or sense of balance has its receptors in the inner ear and senses movement of the head in relationship to gravity. This system tells us if we are moving or still, how fast we are moving, and in what direction.

Your baby senses your movements. It is important to move on a daily basis to develop this system in your baby. Continue to walk, swim, or practice yoga with your healthcare practitioner's guidance.

> The inner ear structure and vestibular balance system form at 8 weeks gestation.

Journaling Reflections

When did you notice some of the first little flutter movements of your baby in utero?

_____
_____
_____
_____

When is your baby active?

_____
_____
_____
_____

How does he/she respond when your body is active?

_____
_____
_____
_____

The Sense of Hearing

By 28 weeks gestation, the cochlea in the inner ear are functioning. Sounds coming from the outside world spark tiny hair cells in the inner ear, sending signals to the brain to interpret sound.

Studies indicate that reading to babies in utero increases their ability to calm.

Babies are able to create memories of stories read to them in utero. After birth, they recognize familiar voices from their womb experiences.

Consider playing your baby's favorite song during childbirth.

Journaling Reflections

What are your favorite stories to read to your baby? How does he/she respond?
_____
_____
_____
_____

What is your favorite music to share with your baby? How does he/she respond?
_____
_____
_____
_____

What are your favorite messages to share with your baby?
_____
_____
_____
_____

The Sense of Sight

By 29 weeks gestation, the visual system is recognizing black and white shades. Cells are beginning to be wired to interpret color.

At birth, your baby is able to see obscure forms and follow motion.

At the age of 3 months, your baby sees more defined edges of images.

By the age of 6 months, your baby sees detail and has clear vision.

Journaling Reflections

A person's name reflects
connection to his or her identity
and individuality.

Calling in a Name

A Name is a Container to Reflect Your Inner Qualities

Listening for Your Baby's Name

Consider the idea that your baby's soul has identified several names to align with its life mission. These names will be subtly communicated with you through messages and signs. Take time to listen deeply and allow the name to reveal itself.

Settle into your sacred space.

- ♥ Begin your naming ritual with a prayer and intention to name your child with a positive name that aligns with his/her soul energy.
- ♥ Research meanings of names.
- ♥ Ask your baby for insights into the name he/she would like to be called. Listen into dreams and messages for guidance on your baby's name.

Journaling Reflections

Notes on your baby's name:

When a woman feels confident in her body, well-supported and uninhibited, she can respond instinctively from her own resources using breath, sound, and movement, optimizing the function of her birth hormones to support a positive birth experience.

—Dr. Sarah Buckley

Beginning or Expanding a Family

Often, there are incredible changes happening in parent and sibling roles and family dynamics when bringing a new, little one into the world. Clear communication at this stage is important for parents to have the best possible start when beginning or expanding a family.

Pre-Baby Discussion Questions for You and Your Partner

- ♥ What is your plan for handling sleep deprivation?
- ♥ Who will be up with your baby at night and provide night feedings?
- ♥ What is the role of grandparents in your family?
- ♥ How will you honor healthy relationships with extended family members?
- ♥ What do you know about post-partum mental health? Up to 1 in 7 women experiences post-partum depression.
- ♥ How will you talk about your mental health needs after your baby is born?
- ♥ Who are the people in your extended support system?
- ♥ Contact a healthcare provider if you have concerns about depression.

Journaling Reflections

The Partner's/Coach's Role During Labor and Delivery

Providing safety and protection during labor and delivery is essential for an optimal experience.

- ♥ Discuss ways you can communicate with your partner during labor and delivery. Mama, what do you need from your partner for connected communication?

- ♥ Mama, how do you process in pain and overwhelm? How can your partner support you during this time? What works? What does not work?

- ♥ Partner, how can you provide protection of the "birthing space" and give Mama the space she needs to be present with herself and your baby?

Journaling Reflections

What do You Need for Support?

During labor and delivery:

- Sibling childcare
- Pet care
- To relax, breathe, and focus
- Movement
- Water
- Coaching
- Music
- Imagery
- Emotional support
- Meditation
- Safety

After your baby comes home:

- Personal care needs
- Childcare needs
- Meal planning support
- Boundaries around visitors
- Grocery shopping
- Rest
- Lactation consultant help
- Household chores and cleaning
- Mental health support

> If you are a trauma survivor, what does your birth team need to know about your needs for consent, choice, and additional safety support?

Journaling Reflections

Birth Plans: Birth Models that Work

Professional and consumer collaboration is an important theme in birth models that work.

—R. Davis-Floyd

> The three primary birth models are:
> - ♥ Hospital birth
> - ♥ Birthing center
> - ♥ Home birth
>
> A one-size-fits-all birth model does not exist.

Natural birth processes optimize mother-parent-baby relationships.

Educate yourself on birth models and which one feels most comfortable and supportive of your needs.

Births don't always go as planned.

Be prepared for a change in plans.
Discuss all possibilities prior to delivery
with your healthcare providers.

Journaling Reflections

My desired birth plan:

_____

_____

_____

_____

_____

_____

_____

_____

_____

_____

_____

_____

_____

Preparing Your Baby for Birth

Settle into your sacred space.

- ♥ Actively talk with your baby and prepare him/her for being released from your womb into the external world.

- ♥ Your baby will lose its womb protective layers.

- ♥ Prepare yourself for releasing your baby from your womb, physically, mentally, and emotionally.

- ♥ It is important that you both begin to think about the concept of birth being the first physical separation of yourself and your baby.

- ♥ Ask your baby to work cooperatively with you through the birth process. Birth is labor; it is active, hard work.

- ♥ Reassure your baby that he/she will be safe and loved in the external world.

Journaling Reflections

The Sacred Hour

The first hour after birth is recognized as the "Sacred Hour."

The Sacred Hour includes:

- ♥ Infant skin-to-skin contact with mother and partner.
- ♥ Delayed cord cutting.
- ♥ Eye-gazing with parents.
- ♥ No separation from the mother unless in a life-threatening emergency for the first hour after birth.

> Raylene Phillips, MD, (2013) discusses the importance of how babies are treated during birth. She says, "Because the first hour after birth is so momentous, we have named it 'The Sacred Hour' at our hospital."
>
> She considers it a sacred union of individuals who have chosen to spend their lives together.

When the practice of no separation
and skin-to-skin contact is honored,
there are:

- ♥ Increased maternal attachment behaviors.
- ♥ Improved infant brain development.
- ♥ Improved infant sleep-wake cycles.
- ♥ Improved initial breastfeeding.

Journaling Reflections

Your baby's sacred birth story:

_____
_____
_____
_____
_____
_____
_____
_____
_____
_____
_____
_____
_____

Journaling Reflections

Your baby's sacred birth story:

_____

_____

_____

_____

_____

_____

_____

_____

_____

_____

_____

_____

_____

Birth Images
(Secure your images here)

Birth Images
(Secure your images here)

Birth Images

(Secure your images here)

Welcome, Dear Little One

You are seen.

You are heard.

You are understood.

You are loved.

References & Resources

Axness, Marcy, PhD. (2017, May 26). *Attuned Conception—A Secret Gateway to a New Humanity*. New Earth Media.

Buckley, S. (2003). "Undisturbed birth: Nature's blueprint for ease and ecstasy." *Journal of Prenatal and Perinatal Psychology and Health* 17 (4) 261-288.

Chamberlain, "Early and Very Early Parenting: New Territories." *Pre and Perinatal Psychology Journal* 12. 2 (Winter1997): 51-59.

Chamberlain, (2013). *Windows to the Womb*. Berkeley CA: North Atlantic Books.

Davis-Floyd, R. (2009). *Birth Models that Work*. Berkeley, CA: University of California Press.

Emoto, M. (2004). *The Healing Power of Water*. India: Hay House Publishers.

Highsmith, S. (2015). *The First Fairy Tale; Book 1: The Adventure Begins*. Salem, IL: Words Matter Publishing.

Highsmith, S. (2018). *The First Fairy Tale; Book II: The Awakening Heart*. Salem, IL: Words Matter Publishing.

Lynn Kent, T. (2011). *Wild Feminine: Finding Power, Spirit and Joy in the Female Body*. Hillsboro, OR: Beyond Words Publishing.

Kluny, R. (2011). *Healing Touch for Babies*. USA: 21st Century Baby Press.

McCarty, W. (2004). *Welcoming Consciousness*. Santa Barbara, CA. Wondrous Beginnings Publishing.

Nine Months That Made You, (2016) Documentary produced by BBC.

Phillips, R. (2013). The sacred hour: Uninterrupted skin-to-skin contact immediately after birth. *Newborn & Infant Nursing Reviews* 13 67-72.

Verny, T. (1981), *The Secret Life of the Unborn Child*. New York, NY: Dell Publishing.

White, K. and Martin M. (2012). "Pre and Perinatal Experiences for Health and Healing: Babies Needs at Every Stage." *Pathways to Family Wellness*. Issue #36. Winter 2012.

About the Author

Donna Seegers Abler, OTR/L, PPNE, earned a BS in occupational therapy from Mount Mary University in Milwaukee, WI in 1984. She graduated from APPPAH Prenatal and Perinatal Psychology Certification Program in 2019. She studies meditation with iamHeart University and is a trained instructor in Calm Birth Prenatal Meditation.

She has a background in preterm neonatal intensive care and infant development. Donna combines years of research-based medical practices with infant massage, Healing Touch for Babies, leading-edge prenatal and perinatal psychology principles, and holistic health and wellness practices.

Donna has been shaped through her own in utero experience and birth story. She has consciously conceived, carried, and grieved a miscarriage. Donna has raised beautiful and thriving young adult daughters. She continues to expand her professional career and lives a rich life as daughter, sister, aunt, mother, soul sister, guide, teacher, and friend to many.

For more information, please visit www.DonnaSeegersAbler.com.

www.ingramcontent.com/pod-product-compliance
Lightning Source LLC
Chambersburg PA
CBHW060941170426
43195CB00026B/2998